GERMAN SHEPHERDS

by Susan H. Gray

Published in the United States of America by The Child's World®
1980 Lookout Drive • Mankato, MN 56003-1705
800-599-READ • www.childsworld.com

PHOTO CREDITS
© ABC Basin Ajansi/Corbis Sygma: 25
© Cindy Charles/PhotoEdit: 27
© Frank Naylor/Alamy: 23
© imagebroker/Alamy: 13
© iStockphoto.com/Guillermo Perales Gonzalez: 19
© Mark Raycroft/Minden Pictures: 9, 11, 21, 29
© PhotoDisc: cover, 1
© Ralph Reinhold/Animals Animals–Earth Scenes: 15
© Tomek Sikora/zefa/Corbis: 17

ACKNOWLEDGMENTS
The Child's World®: Mary Berendes, Publishing Director;
Katherine Stevenson, Editor

The Design Lab: Kathleen Petelinsek, Design and Page Production

LIBRARY OF CONGRESS CATALOGING-IN-PUBLICATION DATA
Gray, Susan Heinrichs.
  German shepherds / by Susan H. Gray.
      p. cm. — (Domestic dogs)
  Includes index.
  ISBN 978-1-59296-965-4 (library bound : alk. paper)
  1. German shepherd dog—Juvenile literature. I. Title. II. Series.
  SF429.G37G73 2008
  636.737'6—dc22   2007023033

Table of Contents

Name That Dog! 4

Max and Hektor 6

Good-Looking and Smart, Too! 10

Good Dog! 14

German Shepherd Puppies 18

German Shepherds on the Job 22

Caring for a German Shepherd 26

Glossary 30

To Find Out More 31

Index 32

NAME That DOG!

What dog came from Germany? What dog started out guarding sheep? What dog does **rescue** work? What dog was once called the wolf-dog? Did you say the German shepherd? Then you are correct!

5

Max and Hektor

Years ago, many people in Europe kept sheep. Dogs guarded the sheep from thieves and wild animals. The best dogs were strong, brave, and quick-thinking.

In the 1800s, a German man became interested in sheepdogs. He was Captain Max von Stephanitz. In 1899, he went to a dog show. He bought a strong, wolf-like dog named Hektor. He changed Hektor's name to Horand. Soon Horand was the father of many puppies.

The map below shows where Germany is on Earth. The map on the right shows a closer view.

Great Britain

Neth.

Belgium

Lux.

France

Germany

Poland

Czech

Slovakia

Switzerland

Austria

Hungary

Slovenia

Italy

Croatia

Bosnia And Herz.

The captain made a list of things he wanted in a dog. He thought dogs should be smart and friendly. He thought they should be brave, strong, and hard working. He looked at Horand's puppies. He chose the ones that fit his ideas. Those puppies grew up. They had puppies of their own. Again, the captain picked the best ones. In time, he had many great dogs. They were called German shepherd dogs.

People all over Europe started getting these wonderful dogs. People from other places wanted them, too. They took them back to their own countries. Today, this **breed** is known all over the world.

Captain von Stephanitz thought dogs should work hard and serve their owners. Dogs that were just cute or friendly were useless to him.

German shepherds are America's third most **popular** dog breed.

German shepherds are very watchful. This one is watching the photographer!

9

Good-Looking and Smart, Too!

German shepherds are powerful. They are full of energy, too. Adults are about 24 inches (61 centimeters) tall at the shoulder. They weigh around 80 pounds (36 kilograms). That is about as heavy as a sixth grader.

These dogs have black noses, dark eyes, and ears that stand up. They look very smart. In fact, they often look as if they are thinking hard.

This German shepherd is enjoying a sunny fall day.

German shepherds have beautiful double coats. The hair close to the body is short and thick. The outer coat has long, straight hairs. The hair on the dog's face is short. The hair on its tail is long.

These dogs can be black, tan, gray, or brown. Some have patches of these colors. Some have areas of white fur. Many German shepherds have a "saddle" pattern. This is a large black patch that covers the back.

In dog shows, dogs stand still while people look at them closely. Most dogs in shows stand with their back legs even. German shepherds stand differently. They stand with one leg forward and one leg back.

You can see the different colors on these three German shepherds.

Good Dog!

German shepherds are **loyal**, brave, and hardworking. They love to be with people. They are especially loyal to their owners. Sometimes they try to protect their owners from strangers. They might even snarl or growl at visitors. But they can learn to accept new people. Once a shepherd likes you, it is your friend for life!

This German shepherd is an important part of his family.

German shepherds are smart dogs. They love to stay busy. They are quick to learn new tricks. They like games that let them run, jump, and burn off energy. They love to walk with their owners. They love to fetch, or catch flying disks.

These dogs get along well with children and other pets. They do best if they are young when they meet them. Sometimes they growl or bark at other animals. Gentle training can make them stop. German shepherds catch on quickly. Trainers do not need to be loud or mean to them.

German shepherds were once called wolf-dogs. But that made people think the dogs were part wolf. No one wanted a wolf for a pet! Calling the dogs German shepherds made them popular again.

This German shepherd loves to play catch on the beach.

German Shepherd Puppies

Most German shepherd mothers have six to nine puppies in a **litter**. Shepherds are large dogs. Their puppies are large, too. Each one is about as heavy as a grapefruit.

The new puppies have round bodies, heads, and **muzzles**. The pups are helpless. Their eyes are still closed. Their ears cannot hear yet. Their legs are not strong enough to carry them. They do not even have teeth. They stay close to their mother. There they are warm and safe.

This German shepherd puppy is just one week old.

In three weeks, the pups' teeth start to grow in. Their eyes are open, and their ears can hear. Their legs are stronger. The pups start trying to walk. They weigh five or six times what they weighed at birth. They still need their mother, though. They might wander away for a short time. But they do not go very far.

A one-year-old German shepherd weighs as much as 70 newborn pups!

The pups keep growing quickly. They play and run around with their brothers and sisters. That teaches them how to get along with other dogs. They start learning about the world around them. Soon they start going farther away from their mother. After eight weeks, they are ready to go to their new homes.

These German shepherd puppies are about eight weeks old.

German Shepherds on the Job

German shepherds make great pets! They do well at other jobs, too. That is because they are smart and strong. They never seem to get tired.

In the 1920s, people saw that German shepherds made great **guide** dogs. These dogs were trained to lead people who could not see. They quickly learned how to guide their owners safely. They could lead them down sidewalks and across streets. Several other breeds now do this work, too. But German shepherds were the first!

This German shepherd is a guide dog. She is helping her blind owner cross the street.

Many German shepherds work as police dogs. They have an excellent sense of smell. They sniff out drugs and stolen items. They catch people who break the law. They are fearless and untiring in this job.

Other shepherds do rescue work. They work in **disaster** areas. They look for people who need help. They search buildings that have fallen down. They hunt for people who are lost or in trouble. These dogs often become heroes for saving lives.

A German shepherd named Pascha is known as a hero. He searched for people in a fallen building in Oklahoma. In Japan, he found people buried by an earthquake. He worked on a rescue team after a Florida storm.

Another word for dog is "canine" (KAY-nine). Police dogs work in "K-9" units.

This German shepherd
is trying to find people
after an earthquake
in Turkey.

Caring for a German Shepherd

German shepherds shed lots of fur. They need **grooming** every day. Gentle brushing or combing gets rid of the old hair. It is also good for the dog's skin. German shepherds often have skin problems. Some have oily or dry skin. Some even get bare spots from scratching. **Veterinarians** (vet-rih-NAIR-ee-unz) know how to treat these skin problems.

This veterinarian is checking a German shepherd's eyes.

German shepherds sometimes have hip or elbow problems. Their leg bones might not fit into their hips correctly. Their arm bones might not fit together well at the elbow. These bone problems can hurt. The dogs can have trouble walking or running. Veterinarians can often help.

German shepherds shed so much hair that some owners call them German shedders!

German shepherds need plenty of exercise. They need to get outside and run around. They should have a large yard to play in. Or they should exercise every day with their owners. Healthy German shepherds can live into their teens. And they are wonderful to be around!

This German shepherd is looking across a meadow.

29

Glossary

breed (BREED) A breed is a certain type of an animal. German shepherds are a well-known dog breed.

disaster (dih-ZASS-tur) A disaster is a happening that causes terrible loss or suffering. German shepherds help find people after disasters.

grooming (GROOM-ing) Grooming an animal is cleaning and brushing it. German shepherds need grooming.

guide (GIDE) To guide people is to lead them or help them find their way. German shepherds were the first guide dogs.

litter (LIH-tur) A litter is a group of babies born to one animal. A German shepherd mother might have eight or nine puppies in her litter.

loyal (LOY-ul) To be loyal is to be true to something and stand up for it. German shepherds are loyal to their owners.

muzzles (MUH-zulz) Muzzles are animals' nose and mouth areas. Newborn puppies have round muzzles.

popular (PAH-pyuh-lur) When something is popular, it is liked by lots of people. German shepherds are popular.

rescue (RESS-kyoo) To rescue something is to save it from danger. German shepherds work as rescue dogs.

veterinarians (vet-rih-NAIR-ee-unz) Veterinarians are doctors who take care of animals. Veterinarians are often called "vets" for short.

To Find Out More

Books to Read

American Kennel Club. *The Complete Dog Book for Kids.* New York: Howell Book House, 1996.

Fiedler, Julie. *German Shepherd Dogs.* New York: PowerKids Press, 2006.

Miller, Marie-Therese. *Search and Rescue Dogs.* New York: Chelsea Clubhouse, 2007.

Russell, Joan Plummer, and Kris Turner Sinnenberg (photographer). *Aero and Officer Mike: Police Partners.* Honesdale, PA: Boyds Mills Press, 2001.

Stone, Lynn M. *German Shepherds.* Vero Beach, FL: Rourke Publishing, 2003.

Places to Contact

American Kennel Club (AKC) Headquarters
260 Madison Ave, New York, NY 10016
Telephone: 212-696-8200

On the Web

Visit our Web site for lots of links about German shepherds:

http://www.childsworld.com/links

Note to Parents, Teachers, and Librarians: We routinely check our Web links to make sure they're safe, active sites—so encourage your readers to check them out!

Index

Appearance, 10, 12, 18, 20

Barking, 16
bravery, 6, 8, 14
breed, 8

Caring for, 26, 28
coat, 12, 26
colors, 12

Disasters, 24
dog shows, 6, 12

Ears, 10, 18, 20
energy, 10, 16, 22
Europe, 6, 8
exercise, 16, 28
eyes, 10, 18, 20

Germany, 4, 6
grooming, 26
as guide dogs, 22

Hair, 12, 26, 28

health problems, 26, 28
history, 6, 8
Horand (Hektor), 6

Intelligence, 6, 8, 10, 16, 22

Jobs, 4, 22, 24

K-9 units, 24

Legs, 12, 18, 20, 28
life span, 28
litter, 18
loyalty, 14

Muzzle, 18

Nose, 10

Pascha (rescue dog), 24
personality, 8, 14, 16
as police dogs, 24
popularity, 8

puppies, 8, 18, 20

as Rescue dogs, 4, 24

Saddle, 12
sheep, guarding, 6, 8
size, 10, 18, 20
skin, 26
smell, sense of, 24
strength, 6, 22

Tail, 12
teeth, 18
training, 16

Veterinarians, 26, 28
von Stephanitz, Captain Max, 6, 8

Weight, 10, 18, 20

About the Author

Susan H. Gray has a Master's degree in zoology. She has written more than 70 science and reference books for children. She loves to garden and play the piano. Susan lives in Cabot, Arkansas, with her husband Michael and many pets.